Art Director: Rita Marshall
Book Design: Stephanie Blumenthal
Text Adapted and Edited from the French language by Kitty Benedict
Library of Congress Cataloging-in-Publication Data
Benedict, Kitty.
Water/written by Andrienne Soutter-Perrot; adapted for the American reader
by Kitty Benedict; illustrated by Etienne Delessert.
Summary: Discusses the physical properties and importance of water and
describes the water cycle.
ISBN 1-56846-039-2
1. Water—Juvenile literature. 2. Water—Pollution—Juvenile literature.
[1. Water.]
I. Soutter-Perrot, Andrienne. II. Delessert, Etienne, ill. III. Title.
QC920.B46   1992
551.48--dc20   92-6929

WATER

WRITTEN BY

ANDRIENNE SOUTTER-PERROT

ILLUSTRATED BY

ETIENNE DELESSERT

CREATIVE EDITIONS

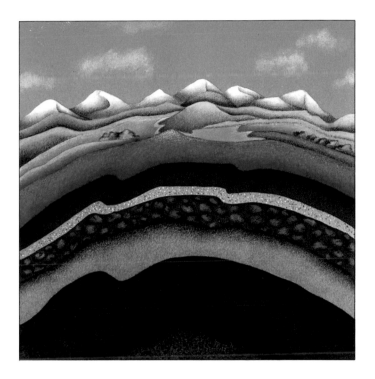

Water is everywhere, all around us.

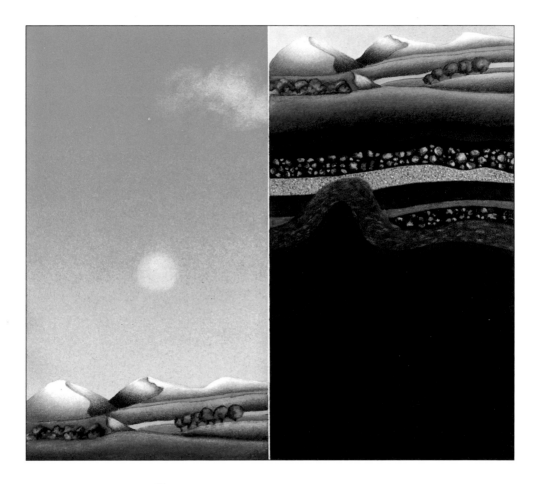

It is in the air and below the ground.

There is water in the flowers, in the grass, and in the animals and insects.

And, of course, there is water in the streams, in the rivers, in the lakes, and in the seas and oceans.

WHAT DOES WATER LOOK LIKE?

Water can be a liquid, like water from a faucet.

It can also be a solid. When water is very cold, it freezes, becoming hard like an icicle.

When water is heated very hot, it boils. A gas made of tiny water droplets rises into the air. We call this steam, or water vapor. Thus, water can be a liquid, a solid, or a gas.

THE WATER CYCLE

The sun's heat constantly draws invisible drops of water into the air. This is called evaporation.

If the air is cool and the earth is warm, these same tiny drops gather to form fog.

Clouds are formed when the water vapor rises high above the earth.

The wind blows the clouds across the sky. When there are many clouds, the sky becomes overcast.

The little drops of water vapor in the clouds join together to make bigger drops. This is called condensation. When the drops grow even heavier, they fall as rain.

When it is very cold, the raindrops turn into ice crystals and fall as snowflakes upon the ground.

When it rains or snows, most of the water evaporates into the air, but some of it runs along the top of the ground, and some of it soaks into the earth.

Underground, the waters collect and sometimes burst out of the land, making a spring. A spring is like a faucet that never shuts off.

The springs form tiny brooks, which run together to make streams.

When many streams come together, rivers are formed.

Some large rivers flow all the way to the seas and oceans.

High up in the mountains, where the snow never melts completely, rivers of snow and ice are formed. These are called glaciers. Like rivers, the glaciers move, but very, very slowly.

During the summer, the warm air melts the glaciers a little bit, and ice-cold water runs down the mountainside.

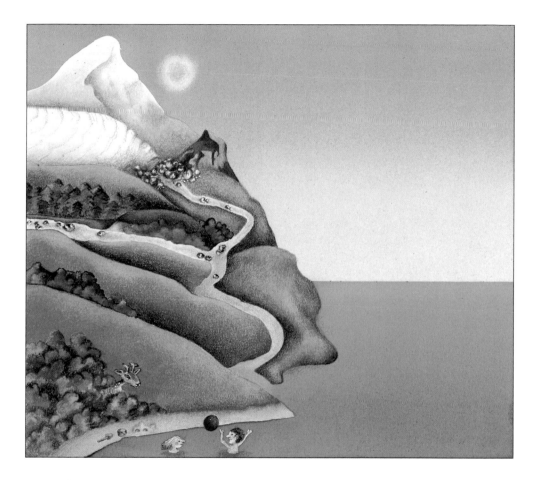

Some of this water joins the streams and rivers, which in turn empty into the lakes, seas, and oceans. The water cycle begins all over again.

WHY DO WE NEED CLEAN WATER?

Most water is clean and pure, whether it is rain, water vapor, or snow.

Sometimes, however, people pollute these clean waters with chemicals and garbage.

All plants need pure water to grow. Without water, they will die.

Animals need clean water, too, whether they live in the water or on the land.

People also need clean water every day.

Even the milk we drink is made of water.

All living things are made mostly of water. Without clean, pure water, there would be no life.